How Children Play

Ingeborg Haller

How Children Play

Floris Books

Translated by Polly Lawson
Illustrated by Almuth Regenass–Haller

First published in German under the title
Das spielende Kind
by Verlag Freies Geistesleben, Stuttgart, 1987
First published in English in 1991 by Floris Books

British Library CIP Data available

ISBN 0–86315–127–2

Printed in Great Britain
by William Collins Sons & Co Ltd, Glasgow

Contents

Developments in Children's Play

Play in Nature

Part One

Developments in Children's Play

1. First Discoveries

The mother is sitting by her child's cot. He is just waking up. Soon he will be wide awake and ready to take the greatest interest in his surroundings. The expectant look in his bright eyes makes his mother wonder what he will be up to today ...

The mother thinks back to her own play days, first of all to the time when she was about eight or nine years old. She remembers how in the first warm days of spring, all the children of the neighbourhood would, without any prior arrangement, gather together and all go off skipping down the street, whirling their skipping-ropes. A week or two later it would be the turn of the brightly painted hoops which they would guide with little sticks along the pavements. Then there were the tops and whips, then hopscotch. On rainy days, they would all meet in one of the houses to roll their marbles in the hall.

In those days, the mother was thinking, nobody told them what games to play. No grown-up said, "Take your skipping-rope with you today." Without any directive the children knew which game they were going to play, in the same way that when it is windy, you know it is a good day for flying kites.

Then the mother goes further back in her memories, but the further back she goes, the less she can remember about the games she used to play, and of course she cannot remember at all what she did when she was only one year old. How is one to know what a one–year–old needs for play?

The mother had already noticed for some time that the soft nappy she had placed beside the cot had become a plaything. Weeks ago the little hands had grabbed it, pulled it up and laid it on their owner's nose covering his face. Soon the little rascal was peeping out of the nappy with one eye while the other half of his face was covered. Perhaps an early form of hide–and–seek? Yes, once the child has really woken up the mother will cover her face with her hands and call, "peep–oh" and see if he likes that game. And sure enough he does. He crows happily and imitates her. This success in bringing joy to her child prompts the mother to observe him more carefully so that she can discover what he needs and so that she can be prepared to meet these needs.

In this way, she starts to see how the little child has his own way of learning. His first years are really expeditions of discovery. The play with fingers and toes is preceded by a "discovery": how far away are those feet that can be felt and grasped but which do not really belong to one's own body? The contented burblings express the satisfaction which these discoveries bring. Lying on his back, the baby pushes his legs up into the air, grabs them and so discovers a part of himself. One hand gropes for the fingers of the other hand; baby examines them carefully, pulls his fingers out a bit, because as yet he has not yet developed all the range of finger movements.

Will the baby need a toy when he learns to sit up? What is he interested in then? His main activity is still grasping. Together with sight and hearing, his sense of touch is engaged in the new discoveries. The hands play with all sorts of shapes and substances: a crumpled up piece of paper (what joy when the child learns to tear a bit off!); or a little saucepan into which a woolly ball is dropped, or smooth rings.

In the old days, children of this age were given wooden dolls without any legs or arms, with only a head and body. The child's hands feel round the head and rounded form of the body, or they grip the body while closely examining the head. A doll like this has no arms and legs to get hold of (to the child who cannot yet stand and walk, legs and arms are not really recognizable, anyway), so the shape of these wooden dolls must be light enough and slim enough to be grasped by the baby's hands. The baby has not yet developed the capacity to be gentle with the doll, so the doll must be strong enough that it will not matter if baby catches it by the head and hammers it against the bars of his cot. Indeed this activity opens up for him a new world of sounds which he himself can produce. Now he notices how paper rustles in his hand, the little bells on his play-pen ring when he touches them, a spoon rattles in a pot, and when he drops something out of his hand, there comes a bump!

How different life becomes for the baby when he learns to crawl. What a joy when he manages to get to where the noise is coming from. The urge to explore makes the crawler want to investigate everything he can see, hear and touch. Now he finds that little tins, pots, boxes with lids are the finest toys;

he opens and shuts them incessantly; and then he pokes something into them and pulls it out again — in and out, two movements that explore the inside and the outside.

When the little child drops his playthings into a pot, then they vanish in the pot and are hidden. They have been swallowed up by the inside of the pot. They have stopped moving; he cannot see their colours any more. If he puts the lid on the pot, everything inside the pot has gone to sleep, but as soon as he lifts the lid all the colours are there again! In go the little hands to grasp the contents and scatter them far and wide, for the "outside" is so wide and so bright while inside the pot the things all lay safely close together.

What is all this: is it exploration, or is it a game? It is both together, for this is how the child to becomes familiar with his surroundings. Everything that is worth discovering becomes a toy: the stockings in the drawer, the sieve in the kitchen, the little boxes with their lids.

For the young child, the sense of touch is as important as the sense of sight is for us. What does the little hand feel when it grasps a wooden ring, and what again when it grasps a plastic ring? Each substance gives out something different. The wood with its firm shape emits not only warmth but aliveness. By contrast, plastic is neutral and cannot be sensed properly, also because its curious lightness in comparison with most natural substances is deceptive: it contradicts the experience gained from natural substances, and children sense this immediately, even though of course not consciously. I have known children, normally careful with their toys, who when they received plastic crockery for the first time, started immediately to throw the plates around and up into the air. They sensed that plastic was too light.

2. A New World of Play

The whole family rejoices when the youngest one learns to stand up on his own for the first time! Beaming all over his face, his eyes sparkling with pride, he has won his way into the vertical. Soon come the first hesitating steps: with raised arms he balances himself. To have mastered the vertical brings with it a new relationship with space. Now arms and hands are no longer needed to crawl along the ground, but are free for a new sphere of play. Soon, as the child becomes more confident of his own balance, he will start to take the blocks out of their basket and start building. In building, he converts the newly won experience of the vertical. It is remarkable with what persistence some children will go on building even though what they build keeps falling down.

The child has great satisfaction if he manages to build a tower taller than himself. Then he reaches up on tip-toe to put yet another block on top, and even drags a chair along in order to climb up and build the tower even higher until in the end it all collapses.

It is good if children have blocks which are not machine-made to set sizes but have thicker and thinner wooden shapes, for example, sections cut from branches. Through using these varied shapes, children get a better feeling of weight and balance, and their experience of the material is more subtle and varied.

The balance which the child has laboriously

achieved in learning to stand and to walk is now projected into the act of building. So now he has to find out: is this block too heavy, that one too small, that other one too pointed? To find the right one requires a lot of trial, and so the child gains varied experience.

The urge to balance goes right through early childhood. The child wants to climb on to every little wall, every fallen tree-trunk. The more a child can practise bodily balance at this age, the better he will be able to find emotional balance later on.

On a rainy grey day, perhaps the child cannot find the right toy or a good corner to play in. With his thumb in his mouth he trots after his busy mother. The mother suddenly thinks of something she has seen in the kindergarten: she places several little baskets and a dish on the child's table, fills the dish half full with walnuts and entices her little thumb-sucker to the table. Then she gives him a wooden spoon and she herself begins to ladle the walnuts from one basket into the other.

Soon the child is busy, ladling and pouring. Meantime his mother has quietly withdrawn. No longer is he a thumb-sucker, but is happily ladling away and pouring away. And he keeps at it for a very long time.

I once saw a family at a bus-stop, father, mother and two girls. Father, mother and the elder girl were sitting on a bench with their hands open on their laps. The younger girl was standing in front of them. She had a coin which she put into her father's hand, and he closed his hand over it. Then she opened her father's hand, took out the coin and put it into her sister's hand who likewise closed her hand. Again the little girl opened the hand, took the coin and put it into her mother's hand. As the game went on the coin went all round the group, sometimes missing out the father, sometimes going twice to the mother and sometimes the sister got it more often than the parents!

Are these a senseless games, this pouring from one receptacle to another and back again, this endless passing of the coin from hand to hand? For a child, it is endless fun to pour water from a bowl into a jug and then into cups, and then pour it back into another bowl and into a tea-pot and out again. We can only be amazed how long two and three-year-olds can keep themselves busy in this way in total contentment. Is this senseless play?

The scene at the bus-stop shows most clearly that here we have to do with an archetypal human gesture: giving and taking. When we visit a family where there is a little child and we bring a gift, the child will often put the gift back in the hand of the giver and then come and take it again in a little while. Giving, and taking so that it can be given again? These are not only archetypal gestures, but they are archetypal rhythms, as breathing in and out.

In this giving and taking we see again the same tireless repetitive activity which we observed as the child learned to crawl, walk and talk. A patience and persistence is at work here which demands our respect and admiration.

In this early stage of play, fundamental human capacities are developed. Little children give away as trustingly as they receive. They are totally absorbed in the process which makes things disappear when they give, and which gives them something when they take. Why do we call giving and taking archetypal gestures? In our social life, we exist by giving and taking. Without these two activities, there would be no education, no trade, no manufacturing, no medicine. A constant exchange of giving and taking is necessary to make our social life possible.

Into these archetypal activities, which the little child so trustingly executes, adult egoism intrudes when taking has the upper hand.

3. "This is My House"

In this activity of giving and taking we see again the same tireless repetitive behaviour which we observed as the child was learning to crawl, walk and talk. Let us continue to observe the young child to see what else their development requires.

I have often found in the kindergarten that the smallest ones would sit under the table over which they had hung cloths, calling for "more, more cloths" till it was quite dark underneath. Then they would sit there quite still, not wanting to be disturbed.

When children create such a "dwelling" of their own, they are perfectly content, while the ready–made playhouses in the garden or in the playroom leave them unsatisfied. This reveals that we grown–ups cannot really tell what "dwelling" the children need or when and where.

Just as we have a feeling of happiness when, after a long walk on a hot summer's day, we come back to the protection of our house, so the child has a need of being enclosed, for he lives all the time "outside" himself entirely in his surroundings, his senses being active beyond measure, so that from time to time he no longer wants to be "outside" but wants to withdraw inside his little house in the dark.

To enable children to "withdraw" there are tables and stands in the kindergarten with all kinds of cloths, large and small, in various colours. These cloths, each dyed in a bright natural colour, are of the greatest importance in any playroom. To enclose himself or a doll, even some object that seems insignificant to us grown-ups, is one of the child's needs. Just recently in the kindergarten I saw a low rectangular object wrapped up which lay on one side all morning. "That's one of our secrets," two of the older children explained. During the last twenty minutes of the morning the children wanted to unveil their long-guarded secret. Two older and two younger girls were involved. And now at last the time had come. The four children carried the "wrapped up thing" into the middle of the circle of the sitting children. Then the outside cloth, the blue one was removed; underneath was a red one, then a green one, then a yellow, another red, then a brown and so it went on. The ceremonial act consisted in removing one cloth after the other, in all eight. The spectators sat absolutely still in wonder. When the last cloth was removed there appeared two wooden animals belonging to the toy-box, and these were sitting on two low stools. The animals did not interest the spectators, what interested them was that one cloth after the other was removed, or in other words they were interested in the process of "unveiling."

Children love wrapping long cloths tightly round themselves (even on hot summer days). The thickness of the cloth wrapped round them, preserves them from too much lightness, from too much transparency. Many children's games which we call "dressing-up" are basically a protection, a kind of second skin. Little children require sheaths, not only physical visible ones, but also invisible ones: soul–warmth, heart–warmth, interest in what they are doing and understanding.

When adults are matter–of–fact, abstract and intellectual, their attitude pulls away the wraps of children and leaves them soul–naked. Just as a bud has enclosed its inner wealth — everything that it is going to bring forth in the future — so little children have to preserve what they have brought with them, so that when the right time comes (that is not too early) their wealth can be revealed.

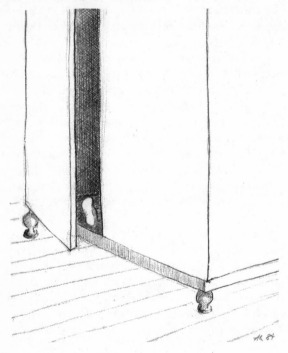

4. Words, Sounds and Rhymes

As soon as the child has learnt to walk, he loves it when grown-ups recite little verses and rhymes with accompanying rhythmical movements. So children love to hear such verses over and over again. Rhymes like this stimulate not only by their sound but also by their rhythm, and also meet the child's need for playing at forming words. How often will a child lie in bed making up things, intermingling what he has heard with what he can create himself, so that something new is always emerging.

The old nursery rhymes offer precisely this sort of rhythmical play to the children, as for example this little Swiss verse:

Hammer, hammer, hammer, bang, bang, bang,
Hammer, hammer, hammer, clang, clang, clang,
Water, water, water, drip, drip, drop,
Wavy, wavy, wave, flip, flip, flop.

Here, if the grown-up not only recites the words but also uses gestures, the child's enjoyment is doubled with hearing and seeing a finger banging on the table, a hand going drip, drip, drop, or doing a wave going flip. It is the gesture which makes the first impression on the child. This is the case also in this little rhyme:

There was a little man
And he climbed in a can,
But when he wanted out
He climbed up through the spout.

Here you can let your thumb crawl into your fist and then crawl out again. It is a game reminding us of the game with the pots and boxes already described, the game of inside and outside.

There are many such verses with gestures to accompany them. Here are a few well–known examples:

Eenie, meenie, mynie, mo
Catch a tigger by his toe,
If he squeals, let him go,
Eenie, meenie, mynie, mo.

One, two, three, four, five,
Johnny caught a fish alive.
Why did you let him go?
Because he bit my finger so.

Here all five fingers come into play as the child catches each finger in turn with his other hand. In the following, the game is with the toes:

This little piggy went to market,
This little piggy stayed at home,
This little piggy had roast beef
And this little piggy had none
And this little piggy went wee, wee, wee
All the way home.

The following example has a whole series of connected hand movements.

> Here is the church and here is the steeple,
> Here are the pews and here are the people.
> Here is the parson going upstairs.
> Here is the parson saying his prayers.

As soon as the child acquires a greater vocabulary he begins to enjoy playing with sounds, making words creatively out of sound. The young child grows into language, and this for him is a creative activity, conducted with any formal knowledge of grammar. He is activated by rhythm and sound and he forms his words by what he hears and by what he invents, as for example:

> a fellytone (a telephone)
> a hostiple (a hospital)
> a dust–tin (a dustbin)
> a toofypeg (a tooth)
> mouth–fur (beard)

Many languages have old verses consisting partly or entirely of phonemes in rhythm without any meaning, such as:

> Ah, ra, chickera,
> Roly, poly, pickena.

Or counting verses such as:

> Eenie, meenie, mackeracka,
> Hi, di, dominacka,

Stickeracka, roomeracka,
Om, pom, push.

Children love it when you let one hand come along
like a mouse and creep into the other with the following:

Hickory, dickory, dock,
The mouse ran up the clock.

And they are full of glee when you take them on your
knee and jog them to the rhythm of a nursery rhyme,
especially when at the right moment after jogging
along there is "an accident" and the rider falls down!

To market, to market,
To buy a fat pig.
Home again, home again,
Jiggety–jig.

Or:

Ride a cock–horse
To Banbury Cross
To see a fine lady
Upon a white horse
With rings on her fingers
And bells on her toes
She shall have music
Wherever she goes.

By rocking the child gently we shake out his powers
and capabilities, freeing sounds and song so that the

child begins in a dreaming way to form words and verses. So a swing can be very stimulating: first a little swing with a cage–seat and then a bigger free swing. The swing allows the child to go up and down in the same rhythmical fashion as in– and out–breathing. This can help children to express thoughts and feelings rhythmically, their first foray into poetry.

Anyone hearing children singing when they are swinging cannot help but swing inwardly with them and feel how speech and song is freed for creativity.

> How do you like to go up in a swing,
> Up in the air so blue?
> Oh, I do think it the pleasantest thing
> Ever a child can do.
>
> Up in the air and over the wall,
> Till I can see so wide,
> Rivers and trees and cattle and all
> Over the countryside—
>
> Till I look down on the garden green,
> Down on the roof so brown—
> Up in the air I go flying again,
> Up in the air and down!

We might go on filling many pages with children's poetry. This kind of rhythmic expression arises spontaneously at moments when children are happy and unencumbered and they are caught up in a rhythmical motion as when on a swing. The mere sound of a word of several syllables can keep children interested for hours once they have found their way into the rhythm of the word. For instance, a little girl on a long train journey, discovered the rhythm of the word *rhododendron* which she kept on repeating dreamily to the rhythm of the train wheels: *rhodo−den−dron, rhodo−den−dron.*

5. The Magic Spell of Imagination

We have seen that the young child's ability to play is constantly changing as he develops. New possibilities arise as he learns to walk and to talk. The following scene is typical of so many. Mother and father had gone for a walk in the woods with their child, and now it was time to go home in the car. The father said: "Come on, now, throw that dirty stick away, you can't take it with you in the car." The child looked at his father reproachfully: "But it's my little dog, he can't stay in the woods all by himself." Further argument only increased the child's distress. In the end he was allowed to take "poor old Scamp" into the car. When they got home the child disappeared into his playroom with the stick. When the mother came into his room later, she was surprised to find that the stick was no longer "Scamp" but had turned into a por-ridge–spoon and the child was now busy cooking supper for the dolls. For some days the stick lay abandoned in a corner until one day it came to life again: this time as a flute.

When we go for a walk, how often do we hear adults saying things like: "Throw away that horrid stick, it's absolutely filthy." The child has just fished it out of the dense undergrowth. Why had the child chosen that particular stick? Certainly not because it was easy to

27

get hold of. But it had to be just that stick because in the first fleeting glimpse of the stick the child's imagination had already transformed it into — well, into what? We grown-ups do not know, but at that moment the stick had become precious for the child, perhaps a living creature, or perhaps just a most desirable object. Of course when the adult enforces his or her commands, the child has been deprived of the power to transform; whatever the stick was going to be has been destroyed.

One needs a loving understanding of children to be able to accept this early creative power — at its strongest between the third and fifth year — which enables them to transform everything that they perceive. For days a little girl carried round a square block wrapped up so that nothing of the block was to be seen. She cared for this block with the greatest devotion. For a time the block was the child's doll which she loved dearly.

If a parcel has been unpacked, the cardboard box can become a desired toy, a doll's bed. Then the box is set up so that little wooden animals can live in it. Later the child attaches a piece of string to it and pulls it along like a sledge, carrying all sorts of things, nuts, shells, little blocks: it has now become a vehicle.

The older the child is, the more play has coherence and sociability. When other children come to play, the games become more involved. The younger child prefers to play with only one other child or person.

A four and a half year old little girl was running through the kindergarten room carrying a doll on a soft cushion in her left arm, while her right hand was holding a short round stick pressed firmly to the doll's mouth: she was giving her baby its bottle.

She was running with the doll to meet her playmate Sebastian. Now she laid the doll on two chairs pushed together while she and Sebastian climbed on to them and danced on top of them. Suddenly the girl jumped down and hauled along a child's bed from the store-room. This she placed beside the tables and surrounded them with stands covered with cloths. It all looked as if she were busy home-making. Even though then for a spectator very little happened after that, a great deal was going on in her imagination. Then off she went with her doll in her arms to play with Sebastian in another corner of the playroom, leaving her "home" empty and unoccupied.

To be constantly active, carried along by an imagination that is always shaping and transforming, is life-elixir for a child of that age. The child will choose for his example only visibly active, visibly creative people. Five-year-olds want to become firemen, bus-drivers or pilots rather than professors!

Do children of this age then require no ready-made toys such as we like to give them for their birthdays or for Christmas? Do children really play only with sticks, logs, tables, chairs and stools? Let us put the question rather differently: what does the child require for play at that age?

We have already seen that when the child is quite free to follow his own bent and is allowed to take what he requires then he will take very simple things, plain "rough-hewn" things. A little stone, a piece of string, a snippet of cloth from mother's work-basket, a bit of gold-paper dropped on the floor: these are the precious things that a child will keep in a pocket for days, while in the playroom the most expensive mechanical construction sets, metal cars of all sizes, and plastic building sets, not to mention the electric train are all left standing around; while in the beds there are dolls that can do all sorts of things, can open and shut their eyes, make noises, even say things and wet their pants. But the possessor of all this magnificence goes and takes a block of wood wrapped in a bit of paper as her doll!

How often do we grown-ups choose a present for a child because we like it ourselves, because we had one like it when we were little, because it is something quite new, and so on. But is it really the toy for the child at his present stage of development? Again we are faced with the question, what does the child require at this age?

A metal car is something perfect in its shape and design. There is only one thing you can do with it, and that is to let it go whizzing about. Can the perfect doll which we have described be happy or sad? No, it has a stereotyped sort of smile. It cannot turn somersaults or climb trees and bushes like the home-made doll. The child's imagination cannot create anything with it.

We must realize that the child lives in a world that is constantly being transformed, into which we cannot enter. The child cannot describe it to us, we can only guess at it through the names which the child gives to the thing: like the name "Scamp" for the stick which became a dog. This world of the child is full of activity. Something is always coming into being, and then being transformed. Living beings come about and disappear again. There are events which only happen for children but which they cannot yet describe, nor wish to, for if once the events were mentioned they would lose their power to be transformed.

The highly imaginative activities of this time will certainly not be impaired but rather enhanced by quite simple, plain toys, which the imagination can make something of. These must be simple, beautiful in form and attractive in colour: wooden animals of various sizes, home-made dolls, plenty of coloured cloths of different sizes; also hobby-horses, balls (large enough not to be swallowed) and little stools, animals on rockers, knitted rabbits, birds, hens, prams, rocking-horses and cradles. Even when children have reached the stage when they can play a real game, planning it and executing it, they still possess some of early childhood's imagination.

Two little sisters, four and five year olds, had been allowed to take part in a little Shepherds' play during Advent. Now they wished to play this Christmas play with their toys. They searched their toy-box and cupboards for a Joseph and a Mary. Finally I heard them call out: "My camel is Mary, and my elephant is Joseph."

As children approach the right age for going to school, their early imagination begins to decline. This imagination which had the power to transform the object-world surrounding the child is now slowly transforming itself within the child. The child's own thinking flashes up, and perception comes more to the fore. The imagination recedes before the perception, but creates picture-images in the child's mind.

A six-year-old girl is watching her little sister among her dolls. She watches her putting little chestnuts into a saucepan. "What are you cooking?" "Potatoes." "What do you mean, potatoes, those are chestnuts, not potatoes." Nevertheless she herself had just been playing with her marbles. The biggest marbles were father and mother, and the others were the children who had been doing all sorts of things. She was at a stage where both her "early childhood imagination" and her developing thinking were present. The marbles she had "transformed" in her own playing, but the chestnuts remained chestnuts and not potatoes to her observation.

Even seven-year-olds can still enjoy "transforming." Some children of this age had built a big ship out of tables, chairs and stools, and had decided to sail off to South America. The grown-up in charge wanted to take advantage of the good weather and suggested that when the ship got to South America the passengers should explore the country round about in the fresh air. Soon the ship tied up at the pier and the gangway was lowered, for they had reached South America!

Everybody left the house and the group set off in the direction of the jungle. On their way they had to pass through streets. The noise of the traffic was transformed by the children into the roars of lions and tigers. At a busy corner they had to cross the street. They looked right and left to see if any danger threatened. All the cars were lions and tigers presenting considerable danger. At last they could cross. Now the way led beside a stream which was turned into a roaring river full of hippopotamuses and crocodiles. In the distance the children caught sight of a tram. "Oh look, now we've seen a camel!" When at last they reached the jungle they could see bananas on the trees, they could hear parrots, and lots of snakes came to cross their path and these had to be killed. Slowly the enchantment of being in an imaginary world faded. The children settled down by a large pond for their morning snack. Soon they were engrossed watching the little frogs and tadpoles hopping about and swimming — they had forgotten all about South America.

Seven-year-olds, ready for school, can decide to play at something together and can carry it through as we have seen with this group. Their early imagination still enables them to enter into the sphere of constant transformation, but now, unlike in their early childhood, they can keep a theme going.

Younger children cannot plan games, nor can they play together on one theme. They follow their sense-perceptions, transforming them immediately. Little children live only in the immediate present, in the moment. The games of older children, accompanied with plenty of chatter and exclamations, are more readily intelligible to grown-ups.

A big seven-year-old girl, holding two four-year-old girls by the hand, said to them: "Now we're going to play at being a family. We've got a three-year-old and a two-year-old and a baby." The three children

33

disappeared into their "house" under the tree, where everything which had been previously planned was now carried out.

Every day for quite a long time, seven–year–old Jock had been arriving first at the kindergarten. He would sit down on a chair as if he were waiting for something. When at last he was asked why he had not started to play he replied: "I have to wait till Jim, Lotty and Paul are here." At last his three playmates arrived. All four now sat together in consultation. Finally a circus was built with a round arena. The main act was the lion who had to jump through a coloured hoop. Then Jim stepped forward as a con-juror. In his hand he held two hazel nuts. Under his arm he had a cloth partly folded and partly hanging down. He waved the cloth a few times over the nuts while he spoke his magic words. Then cleverly holding the cloth so as to pick up one of nuts he lifted the cloth in the air, and one of the nuts had vanished by magic.

With the same trick he made the nut reappear, so that the disappearance was always followed by a reappearance. He went on doing his magic very successfully for a long time while the youngest ones watched him in wonder. But at last Jim had to make way, for the horses were already stamping their feet. Paul, Jock and Lotty had meantime been dressing the hobby–horses with paper cockades between their ears, so that they were now real circus–horses. They went prancing round the arena while the little ones clapped their hands. At last the horses bowed and the circus came to an end.

Admiringly, and full of a desire to be like them one day, the younger children watched the bigger ones who were able to do all these things. Older children can become an authority for younger ones in this way. An older child will often dress up a younger one, then in procession off they go singing between the other groups of children playing and round the room, through the passage and if possible out into the garden.

6. Discovering Weight

Six- and seven-year-olds are often attracted to an object more by its nature and qualities than by what can be done with it. Part of a child's examination of an object is testing its weight. Playing with the object entails trying out the child's own physical powers.

Lightness can be experienced in blowing soap-bubbles, blowing away little feathers, or white dandelion-heads which slowly fall to the ground. Even before they are ready for school, children feel the desire to experiment with weight. Girls and boys have different ways of approaching this. Often six- or seven-year-old girls will persistently carry around a two- or three-year-old even though it is difficult for them, and they stop only when they have grown tired. Boys prefer heavy objects to play with: planks, wooden blocks, tables, chairs and benches. They will climb trees and fix a rope over a stout branch so as to be able to pull up a heavy stone. How heavy is it to pull up? Are we strong enough? How easy is it to lower again?

I once watched a little group of five- and six-year-old boys in a kindergarten garden. They were having a heated discussion. Some days later this group started to work on a heavy hearthstone which lay in a flower bed between rhododendron bushes. Day after day, I watched them at work.

One morning one of the mothers asked me: "What's all this about a stone? At home my son is always talking about a big stone." Well, I wanted to know about it too, so I went and asked the children who were gathered outside.

"Oh, yes," the children answered eagerly. "The stone has got to be moved to the other end of the garden down there in the bushes, but we don't know how we are going to get it there!" I went and got a low but very strong four-wheeled cart and suggested that they transport the stone on the cart. The boys were full of enthusiasm. But how were they going to get the stone on to the cart?

We found a strong plank and a thick rope. We fastened the rope round the stone with some difficulty. Then with everyone pulling their hardest, they were able to pull the stone up the plank and so on to the cart. Then the boys shouted with joy, but jubilation reached its peak as the heavy stone was wheeled right through the garden, some pulling and some pushing. Once we reached the bottom of the garden, the stone had once again to be dragged out with the rope. After the work was completed, the boys stood reverently round the stone — and then ran happily away. After that no one looked at the stone, no one even talked about it: interest in the stone had ebbed away.

Tackling weight in this way strengthens the limbs, the foot treads more firmly, and such self-imposed tasks strengthen the child's confidence in his own powers.

Airiness draws everything upwards. Children who are too much given over to this element walk on tip-toe and speak with a piping voice out of the head. They need to play with heavy things.

At the beginning of the stone episode, it was important that I had *not* asked the children *why* they wished to move the stone. The children could not have given a reason, and it would only have distracted them from their purpose. The real reason was that they were living out an inner need, for the need to tackle natural objects lies deep in the child's sense of living; this need has not risen into his consciousness and so it cannot be discussed.

7. Learning through Imitation

From the moment when children can crawl or walk to whatever attracts them, they like best to be where they can watch some activity. Wherever mother or other adult is busy all morning, the little child wants to be there, too. And soon they will be saying: "Me too," meaning that they want to help. An understanding adult will allow children to be there and let them "help" as much as possible.

Two little sisters, a two–year–old and a three–year–old, saw a bucket of water standing in the kitchen corner, ready for use, which their mother had put ready before having to hurry out into the garden to get the washing in. The floor–cloth was lying beside the bucket. Quickly the two little helpers got to work, slopping lots of water over the floor with the wet cloth and leaving puddles everywhere. Then they found the mop and pushed it into the bucket with such force that it was knocked over and flooded the kitchen just as their mother came back.

Every mother has stories of this kind to tell. Sometimes three– and four–year–olds manage to give their parents a surprise, when for example on a Sunday morning, before the parents have risen, the children have laid the breakfast table. They carefully do everything just as their parents do.

The more children imitate adult work-activities, the more it is noticeable how closely they have observed how tools are used and how accurately they imitate the manual motions. If two little sisters of three and four have just had a little brother, they will try to look after their dolls in exactly the same way as their mother looks after their little brother. The doll is wrapped in nappies, and of course it has to be bathed, fed and, later, while little brother is being weaned, taught how to eat from a spoon.

One summer's day something was going on outside the kindergarten. Children from higher up in the school appeared in the garden with their teacher and an architect. They were going to build a little baking oven with bricks and mortar, under a clump of trees. The kindergarten children were allowed to watch. The grown-ups mixed the mortar expertly and showed the school-children how to apply the mortar to the bricks. The school-children took turns to mix the mortar, to lay it on, and then to lay the bricks, the grown-ups showing them how to do it all the time. Even though the work went on for several hours, the little ones remained fascinated. They were coaxed inside for their morning break, but rushed out again immediately afterwards. Sometimes they sat down on the grass for a bit, but then stood up again in order to see better. When the parents came to collect the little ones, they found it hard to drag them away from watching the work.

Next morning when the kindergarten children ran out to play in the garden, they found to their great joy that a whole lot of bricks had been left over. These "valuable" objects they now took to the sand–pit. In the sand–pit they dug a pit, filled it with water and this was their mortar trough. They took sticks to stir the mortar with. Slowly they poured sand into the water and stirred it in the same way that they had seen the grown–ups doing it the day before. Indeed in the children's imitation I could recognize the teacher's posture as he stirred. At last the mortar had attained the right consistency. As the children worked in the sand–pit spreading the "mortar" on the bricks, I could recognize the hand–movements which I had observed in the grown–ups the day before. Just as on the previous day the children had been completely absorbed in watching the work, so now they laid their bricks with the same concentration.

Now instead of doing what they usually did, making an oven, a house or a castle, they only wanted to do what they had seen. For the day before they had not only observed the interesting processes with their eyes, but they carried out inwardly, unseen by the grown–ups, all the gestures and actions and even the postures. They became inwardly the workers themselves; indeed we might say that they had identified themselves with them in their movements, actions and postures. If a particular child becomes fascinated over a period by a grown–up at work, the child's imitation can go so far as to pick up even the adult's manner of speaking.

One summer's day I was standing with a four and a half year old boy by one of the little ports along Lake Constance. We were watching a small sailing boat coming up to its moorings. Suddenly the boat capsized and lay flat on the water. My little companion watched in suspense how the two young men standing in the water started to right the boat, one pushing up and the other pulling it over. The child watched with fascination as the boat gradually came upright. Every time it sank back again my little friend heaved a sigh, but when at last the boat was righted he had so identified himself with the young men — for he still watched as they unrigged it and snugged it down — that he watched them going ashore and begged me to take him to visit them. After a brief search we found their caravan, and met them now dry and changed at their evening meal. The child stayed sunk in observation for a long time before he could be persuaded to come home with me.

All very young children have an irresistible urge to identify themselves with visible work-movements and processes, which they try to imitate in their play. This identifying includes the actor who is the exponent of the activity.

A little girl had been to the hairdresser with her mother. A few days later she was playing at hair-dressing with her friend. The customer was offered a seat, and a large white cloth was spread round her. The hairdresser now began to brush and comb. The bottle was made of paper rolled up and dripped invisible soap that was massaged into the head. The little hairdresser missed out the rinsing of the hair, and because she had no hair-dryer she rubbed the customer's hair dry with a towel so that she could brush and comb again — her favourite activity.

One day a six-year-old boy asked his teacher for a very long piece of string. He went into the garden with the longest one he could get. This he tied to a post opposite the back door, but he tied it so low down that he could pull the string over the ground to the doorway where he again tied it to a convenient nail. When he had finished he said: "Yesterday the electrician came and laid a cable to our house!"

A six-year-old girl went to a church service with her mother for the first time, and listened to the sermon. Some time later — being one of the older children in the kindergarten with a certain authority over the younger ones — she arranged a number of the children's chairs in a half circle, and made the other children sit down. She placed a table in front of the chairs and on the table was placed another chair. Then she dressed up as the clergyman in a black robe. In her hand she took the smallest picture-book that she could find. When she took up her position in front of the children, they all began to sing a kindergarten song which they all knew, but with a kind of amazement at the new situation. Now the clergy-woman climbed up on to the chair, then on to the table, and finally into her pulpit, where she stood, opened the book and read: "Once upon a time long, long ago there was a wolf and a little kid." Then came a little pause, she climbed down again, and once more the song was sung. The church-goers dispersed quickly and the chairs were quickly removed.

This shows clearly how actions are registered and

imitated by children. The little girl had experienced deeply the actions of the clergyman: the singing, the climbing up into the pulpit, carrying and opening the book, and climbing down again, all this in front of a silent congregation. The spiritual–intellectual part of the service cannot in any way touch children in their first seven–year period.

If you watch children at play day after day, you soon realize how varied are the subjects of their play, stimulated by all that they can find to imitate. Sometimes it is the dentist looking into his patient's mouth, or the dustman carrying the heavy dustbin to the dustcart, or again the postman posting the letters through the letter–box. All these games are filled with observations which the child has made himself. Adults such as the dentist or doctor can play an important and sympathetic part in this process.

Games of this sort should never be subject to outside influence or even performed on request. They have their own laws too: as we have seen the young child first wants to take part and then to imitate. The older the child, and the more he can grasp complicated processes, the longer the interval between the experience and the subsequent enactment. It may be just one day, but it can be several days, even weeks or longer. Just think how annoyed many grown–ups become when children start acting Christmas plays or singing carols in the middle of summer.

Through play the child is preparing for life, and within this activity they need the adult — the whole human being — as example. It is the activities of adults which they can imitate freely, creatively and repetitively. Nothing else, no technology, can replace this example. Nor does the little child learn by listening to carefully thought-out explanations. These are not only unnecessary but moreover an impediment.

8. Hide-and-Seek

We have seen that as children grow older, the manner of their play moulds itself according to each phase of their development. Now there is one game in particular which starts in the cradle and goes on right through childhood, developing and manifesting itself in various ways right up into puberty. That game is "hide-and-seek." Latent in the nature of every child is the desire to seek and find, and this desire is nurtured through increasingly complicated and exciting forms of the "hide-and-seek" game.

At the beginning of this study, we saw how the mother was playing "peep-oh" with her baby as he lay in the cot. In time the baby learns to walk, and now feels sure on his feet. He loves to run from one corner to the other; and especially he likes it when we hide with him in one corner, telling him in a whisper to be quiet while another child starts looking for him noisily.

It is not long before the child learns to hide all by himself. Suddenly he runs out quite unexpectedly from his hiding place laughing and shouting: "Here I am!"

The child has not yet connected the two elements of the game, "hide-and-seek" and "hide-and-find." He still likes to hide in the same place each time. For the time being he is quite happy with "not being there" and then suddenly "being there again," so that

47

it is a game of disappearing and reappearing in constant alternation, played by one person.

If all the children are playing hide–and–seek in the garden, the little one hangs on to his elder sister's hand and is swept along in the excitement of the game. Obediently he squeezes himself behind the wooden seat in the summer–house along with the bigger children, for there the elder sister is convinced that "no one will find us." The excitement of "will he find us, won't he find us" is not yet experienced by the two–year–old; he just does what his sister does.

Once the child is nearing or has reached his fourth year, his play becomes much more varied. Meantime he has had his first encounter with the forces of his own personality, with his I, during the emergence of his own self–will, a period when his conscious experience starts to disengage from his surroundings. With this stage, quite new abilities awaken, and now he sees that to hide in order to be found, and to seek in order to find are really two quite different, indeed quite opposite actions. The child will only be able to make a connection between both experiences after the age of three, and the older kindergarten child has in fact just as much pleasure "finding" as he used to have at "coming out and showing himself."

Once I was going home from a playground with a group of twenty children. In order not to keep the parents waiting, we had to hurry. The way home led through a meadow lined with tall trees with thick trunks. I ran ahead and turning round to the children running after me I shouted, "Find me" and hid behind a tree. All the children ran to the tree and shouted

Name _____
                    Surname

Address _____

_____

_____
                    Postcode

If you are interested in
other publications from
Floris Books, please
return this card with your
name and address.

☐ Please send me your catalogue once

☐ Please send me your catalogue regularly

☐ Please send me a sample of *The Threshing Floor*, bimonthly journal of
The Christian Community — movement for religious renewal

Postcard

Floris Books
15 Harrison Gardens
EDINBURGH
EH11 1SH
Great Britain

joyfully on finding me, nor was their delight any less as I repeated the game from tree to tree until we got back.

Primary school children tend to look for more and more difficult challenges. "Hiding, seeking, finding" eventually becomes too simple, too straightforward. It needs a new component. So at a certain stage other elements are added, for example a "home base" which can be a tree, a summer-house or just a piece of ground marked by a stick. You are "safe" if you have left your hiding place and reach "home" without being caught by the one who is "it."

This increases the fun. Hiders and seekers are now in constant excitement. The one hiding peeps through a chink in his hiding place, listens for the steps of the seeker, for he must seize on the right moment to run. Perhaps the seeker suddenly appears from behind a bush where she thought someone might be hiding, catches sight of the hider running to the "home base" and catches him at the last moment. But only when she has caught all those who were hiding is she the winner.

As the children grow older, this game of hide-and-seek with a base can develop into a game of "Soldiers and Robbers." For this game the best place is a wood with undergrowth and a clearing. This is the robbers' castle. It is a game with sides. One side, the robbers, have their headquarters in the robbers' castle; the other side, the soldiers, hide in the wood where they can be found and caught by the robbers. But now there is a new twist to the old game. The robbers' prisoners can be freed by touching them. For this the soldiers who

49

are still free need to creep right up undetected, while of course those in the robbers' castle keep a good look-out, but also must sally forth to capture more prisoners. So the excitement is increased beyond that of hide-and-seek with a home base. You must wait for just the right moment when the attention of the look-outs is distracted by soldiers spotted in the woods and then you can dash in and rescue a prisoner or two. If the raid does not go according to plan, the raiders may be captured while the old prisoners succeed in escaping. This game can go on for hours as the fortunes of either side go up and down.

In hide-and-seek the younger child lives completely in the rhythm of disappearing and appearing, but older school-children need something more than that. For these, it is through the excitement of the more developed games that they acquire the self-awareness necessary at their stage of development. As the soul becomes excited, the breathing is enlivened and, as the excitement ebbs away, grows calm again. Children who regularly experience this sort of game become healthier for it.

Part Two

Play in Nature

9. Experiencing Water and Rain

Young children live close to nature. They long to make the water–element their friend and playmate in all its forms: as ice or rain, as flowing stream or calm sea, as ebb and flood of the tide, or as the ever–gushing fountain.

Yet water is very mysterious for the young child: how quickly the icicle melts which only a little while ago was hanging from the roof glistening in the sunshine. The child's small hand scoops up water, but the water does not stay there: it runs out through her fingers. And how mysterious it is to look down into water. The depths are so very dark, while the heavens are reflected on the surface, and the child discovers her own reflection there. Or the experience of rain: how quickly it can change the child's world! The rain creates the puddles, those miniature lakes in the street and on the pavements. In the garden, there are rain–drops everywhere, glistening like pearls; and when the children see the bush or tree with all the tiny drops on its branches they cry out: "Look, it's got flowers."

There is an old German country saw which describes the rain as a friend to children:

> Rain in May brings joy to earth
> So if on us it shower,
> We too will gladly grow
> Like grass and flower.

Many happy and instructive hours can be spent by children playing by a brook, enjoying its little water-falls and currents. How interesting it is, too, at the seaside, to watch the tide coming in: a few hours ago you had to walk out a long way to reach the sea and now it has come right in and has devoured everything the children built of sand.

This ever-flowing, changing element which you cannot hold with your hands is the young child's favourite element. But here too they cannot articulate what water means to them. Only by watching carefully can the adult sense what the elements mean to the child. Some of this meaning comes through in the writings of Stefan Andres, who describes how he played beside the millstream in his early childhood:

I loved the water behind the low wide wall of sandstone where the women washed their linen or sat chatting. I did not abandon myself entirely to the water by stepping into it, but leaning over the smooth stone wall with my smock sleeves rolled up I would dip my arms into the water and gently stir and caress it. Nikla too used to play beside me with the water. The game was simply to stir the water with our arms. I tried to catch it in both arms, but it just spilled away. You could feel its weight but only for a moment. I loved the feeling of the smooth body of the water held in my arms until they hurt with the cold and grew red and stiff. And then there was the light on the water, the sky breaking into little bits, and suddenly a bit of a face that wavered and floated away. There were moments of fright and delight and then forget-fulness flitted over my eyes, and a state of pure bliss was there again. The water was smooth, cool, it moved so beautifully and held me fast, until my father came to fetch me home. Gradually the water had taken possession of my whole little person, and it was a wonder that I did not have a cold all the time!*

The author describes the pure bliss he felt when he was playing in the water with his arms and hands. Even a puddle can bring out similar feelings in a small child when the tiny bare feet step into it, or when they splash the water as they run through it.

Puddles can also stimulate extended and thoughtful play. In our town there is a quiet little square with a chapel under tall old lime-trees. After a heavy thunderstorm in the night a big round puddle had formed not far from the chapel wall. The three-year-old girl living nearby regarded the puddle as the sea. She squatted on the seashore. The ground under the limes was strewn with round seeds with stalks and wings. The child picked up one seed after the other and launched them as ships on the sea. She went on playing there for a long time quite absorbed and did not let herself be disturbed by the passers-by who stopped to look at her. She hardly noticed them. More seeds with stalks and wings came floating down, borne by the gentle breeze.

The rain that fills the countryside with puddles and sometimes leaves bright droplets hanging in the air, often makes a child pensive. A little group of children were standing by the window looking out at the rain. They were watching everything getting wet outside:

* From: *Der Knabe im Brunnen* [The Boy at the Well].

"Look, the houses, the cars, the dogs," until a five-year-old said: "The rain can't get things any wetter now. It's raining on itself now." A four-year-old asked his mother: "How does God make the rain?" Before his mother could answer, the boy exclaimed: "Oh I know how, he takes a big tin and makes a whole lot of holes in the lid. The tin is always full of water. When it is time for the rain, God turns the tin upside-down, and holds it over where the earth has to be wetted. And that's how it rains."

We see how the phenomenon "rain" always stirs the child's soul. Of course two and three-year-olds do not make up such thoughtful observations which explain the world. The little ones who by nature want to hold and touch everything, have to feel water, rain and earth through their sense of touch. They have to play with it until they are quite familiar with it.

10. Water and Earth

When water and earth are mixed, the child is stimulated to play particularly by the sense of touch. It
makes a difference whether children play with water
and sand or with water and earth. Sand is lighter and
runs through the fingers. It is more granulated and
more mineral. Earth is heavy and dark. What we call
"mud" is when earth is mixed with water. Who does
not remember the secret excitement when your bare
feet trod in the squelchy mud and it came oozing up
through your toes? It was very pleasant to feel this
wet soft squishy substance. This is the substance
which the child needs in order to create forms. The
actual forms created are not so important; what is
important is the creative activity.

James had discovered a mole heap in the little field
in front of the house. He fetched some water to work
the dry earth into a workable consistency. When the
earth was soft enough, he made mud-pies out of it in
shapes which suited his tiny hands. Then he left his
little creations to dry in the sun. How surprised he was
when his soft material grew as hard as a rock, so that
it could be pulverized and finally broken up.

When the children call out: "Mummy, we're going
to play in the mud," all she needs to do is to make
sure that they take off their shoes and stockings, roll
up their sleeves and put on a plain apron. Just as when
we are baking, the right mixture of earth and water

must be made up. The children have filled an old basin with earth, and now they are going to add water, and already their arms and hands are stirring. The stuff is still too solid. They shout, "More water!" and out of the watering can comes the necessary liquid, just like mother baking in the kitchen. Now the dough has to be kneaded: this is the main activity for the children. More and more "dough" is mixed until all sorts of cakes and balls are spread out on a large board. Once done, everything is left on the board to dry ... and interest fades.

In a meagre little garden, right in the middle of the town traffic, four children used to gather for a session of what they called "smirgling." In this bit of ground there were not many plants growing, and one side was shut in by a high wooden fence. In spite of the poor soil, the earth could be loosened and, in a hollow under the swing, it was moist and fine-grained. This hollow now served as a big basin: water lay already to hand in an old watering-can. The children began to feel the moist earth. They took a lump out here and there until one of the children began to roll the earth between his hands, and soon he had made a nice round ball. Very soon the other children followed suit and soon there was a whole lot of smooth round balls collected in a heap. Next day the balls were forgotten.

This garden incidentally did not look at all like a nice playground. Even so the children spent their most important playing time there, busying themselves with the primal elements of our existence; water and earth, mixed and formed into the primal shape of the sphere.

The children's sense of touch could unite itself with both elements and create a feeling of wellbeing.

Many people question playing with water and earth. "Isn't it enough if they have a sandpit?" I am often asked. Or: "Do they have to play with this muck?" Earth is not muck or dirt, it is the foundation of our nature to which plants, flowers and trees and human beings belong. The earth offers itself to us so that we may walk upon it. Therefore it is fitting that the child should touch it, feel it so as to test its consistency, and finally work with it and shape it. Children want to know the earth and want to love water. Inevitably they will get dirty, but is that a bad thing so long as they wash and scrub their nails afterwards? Children who are fortunate enough to be able to play with water and earth will not later become people who will only touch things with their finger-tips, who do not want to dirty their hands. They are the lucky ones who have plunged their hands firmly into water and earth and enjoyed all the subtle differences of substance and consistency.

11. Stream and Stones

Young children when they are allowed to play in these elements need very little: to play with water, two little pots and a jug are enough. The three–year–old will sit on the sea–shore, fill the jug and pour it all over himself, then he stands up and once the jug is filled again he pours out a thin water–spout into the sea. First sitting and then standing, the child makes the stream of water first short, then long; and so it continues. These are new experiences which are often carried on in the bath in the evening.

Then there are the stones beside the river, lake or sea, enticing the child to new experiences. Little stones go plop and disappear almost as soon as they are thrown in. The child however loves the rings they set up on the surface. He fetches bigger and bigger stones. They splash into the water, and the big heavy ones make a new noise. Later, father shows the children that he can make flat stones skip across the water.

Children love to return to the places where they have played before. The place has become familiar to them, however small it may be, and they feel at home. They know where to find the loveliest stones; they know the tree where they have built a den; all is familiar, the bushes, the pond, even the occasional visiting cat. To feel absolutely at home, doing the same things in the same place is very good for young children. Therefore a garden is very important in so far as the children are allowed to play in it. So too returning regularly to the same holiday house fosters the feeling of familiarity as each time the old well-known objects are greeted with joy.

And if there is a stream or brook in the neighbourhood, it soon becomes the favourite place for playing. With every fibre of their being the children can experience the flowing streaming element. As they cannot themselves be borne away by the current, they feel the living urge to find something — even if it is only a long stalk — to let the current carry away. The children feel the desire to be giving the brook something to carry away all the time.

They can experience, too, how the stream changes over the seasons of the year! In winter lumps of ice go floating down; you can break off gleaming icicles, and suck them. In spring, all that has disappeared; the brook is free of ice, and flowers blossom in the grassy banks. In summer, there is not so much water — the brook has become a little trickle! Then the autumn rains fill it again and it begins to carry lots of fallen leaves in it, until finally in the deep cold of winter it is covered with ice once more.

Near our kindergarten there is a little river coming from the Black Forest and flowing towards the town. On one side there is a wood and on the other there is a pleasant path going along the banks past some gardens. I used to go to this stream with the older children to find a place to play. When the children were smaller they had played in the garden with water and earth. Now they were going out to make new discoveries and new experiences. In my notes for the middle of January, I find the following:

It is a day of sunny winter weather. As we approach the stream the hoar-frost is glistening on the trees, on the bushes and on every blade of grass. Above the little waterfall at the edge of the stream, there are thick and thin sheets of ice which the children break off. Now with cries of delight they run along the banks back to the waterfall to hear the noise when the ice plunges down with the water. It is a deep booming noise. Now we need a lot of strong sticks to free the lumps of ice which have got stuck. Thomas finds a very suitable iron rod while the others collect more or less suitable sticks. With these the children are able to break off a number of the ice lumps. Christine is beaming with delight: "It's lovely here, it's lovely here," she shouts all the time.

Another note from the end of February:

Today is a mild sunny day with spring in the air, and the birds are chirping. The children are glad because they can go to the stream again, and so we get there quickly.

Just above the waterfall the children find two thin flat pieces of wood in the water, probably the bottoms of cigar boxes. But both little "boats" get stuck in the bushes at the edge of the waterfall. Thomas and Stephen who have wellington boots on, step into the water and fish two sticks out. To the cheers of the children on the bank, Stephen manages to free one of the little boats. Christopher is lying on his tummy on

the bank and gets Thomas to fish a thick long branch
out of the water for him. Christopher then manages to
free the second boat from above. The branch is only
just long enough and Christopher has to slide forward
a long way to be able to reach it. But he manages it.
Of course when this second boat sails free, all the
children cheer again.

A note from the end of May:
When they were told, "We're going to the river,"
the boys all shouted with joy. A whole lot of little bits
of wood from Class 12's woodwork lie in one corner
and each child is now allowed to go and choose a
piece to take with him as a boat. Each bit of wood
gets a nail and a piece of string tied to it. Then off we
go at top speed as we have only just an hour before
we have to be back again. Once we reach the water—
fall we set up a little workshop on a stone, as not
every piece of wood has got a nail and string. Then
the hammering begins, while the children, mostly
kneeling, work away with the water rushing below
them.
When Daniel launched his boat he let go of the
string for a moment and the boat got carried away by
the current. Fortunately our way home follows the
stream down. The children run along the bank after
the boat and soon overtake it. Then they stop and
shout, "It's coming, it's coming!" Daniel has armed
himself with a big stick to stop the boat if necessary.
But the children are now again well ahead of the boat
and looking back, they shout, "It's coming, it's com—
ing!" When it really does come and Daniel wants to

stop it, alas his stick and the other children's sticks
are all too short and the boat sails past. Once again
the children rush after it and get ahead of it. Then we
see a little dam consisting of plants and flowers which
have drifted together.

We stop and are convinced that here the boat will
get stuck. It is coming nearer and nearer. Then
suddenly it stops although it has still some distance to
go before it reaches the dam. Soon we see that the
boat's string has got caught on a stone in the middle
of the brook. Thomas says to Daniel: "Give me your
wellies, and I'll go into the water and get your boat
out." No sooner said than done. The boots are
exchanged and Thomas steps into the water while the
other children watch in suspense. The water is shal-
low and Thomas' boots are high enough. He seizes the
boat, pulls the string which immediately comes
unstuck and out they both come, Thomas and the
valuable bit of wood. Boots are given back again and
then we hurry back to the kindergarten.

A note from the beginning of June:
More new experiences. Meantime the children have
improved their boats, and according to their ideas
made them more beautiful, some of them having sails.
Some with the help of elder brothers even have a rail.
The children are looking forward to the day when they
can sail their boats on the water. At last the joyful
day comes. Sunshine and a fresh warm breeze. While I
am going along the garden fence Björn and Mark
come running towards me so quickly that I can
measure their expectations by their legs. As soon as

67

everyone has got their boats we rush off to the stream. Some of the boys run on ahead. They cannot wait. When we get there the event of the day has already begun: Stephen has already let his boat go over the waterfall, but the force of the water has broken the string. Furthermore the cascade has thrown his boat over to the other side and now it is going round and round and is not being carried any further. Unfortunately none of the sticks at hand is long enough, so for the time being we are forced to watch what the water is doing with the boat without ourselves being able to do anything. All the other children are sailing their boats a good bit above the waterfall, and are cheering away. Daniel, Andrew and Martin have tied their strings to posts on the bank so that their boats cannot come adrift and now the boys are clapping their hands with pleasure to see how sea–worthy their boats are.

After a time I notice by chance that a man is opening the gate of his allotment behind us. I quickly ask him for a long rake to fish Stephen's boat out of the whirlpool. "I'll get it out for you," he says kindly, and comes with a long hoe. But even that is too short. Then the man says, "I'll tie a pole to the hoe!" Then right enough he reappears with a pole from his garden and goes with his lengthened hoe to the water. All the children come and stand round him. But the stream is still too wide and he cannot reach the boat.

"I'll go and put my boots on," he calls. "That'll do the trick!" He disappears into his shed, and then reappears with wellingtons, picks up his long pole and steps into the whirling water. Three times the good

old man tries before he manages to reach the boat and pull it by the string to the bank. When I thank him gratefully, he says good—bye with the words: "For children I'll do anything."

Last entry: Leaving the stream.

After the summer holidays, all these children will be going up into the main school. So one hot summer's day we go together to the stream for the last time. Now the children are going to get their midsummer's experience by the stream.

The summer day is hot. On the way Mickey, Thomas and Christopher have disappeared because they want to wade along the stream—bed under the road bridge. Now at last they are climbing up the other side. Stephen meets the three of them in the park and says: "I couldn't have done that!"

Now we hurry to reach the first steps leading down into the stream. There we take our shoes and socks off and wade barefoot into the water. Suddenly Elsie slips so that her dress and pants get a bit wet. This little accident has upset her so much that from now on she prefers to stay on the bank. Andrea is paddling about a bit in the water but rather cautiously. Martin on the other hand is jubilant, he does not mind how much he slips and gets wet.

Christopher and Thomas have again discovered another ploy. They have found a tin lid in the water near the bank. They put it in the water above the bridge and let it float down with the current under the bridge. Then they wade out and catch it as it comes along, and start the game all over again. But the second time the current is too strong for them and the tin lid is carried past before they can reach it. But the two boys are so happy paddling that they start singing songs together.

Now we decide to go part of the way home paddling along the stream. But most of the children do not have the courage to wade under the bridge although Christopher and Thomas have already done it twice. Everyone except these two now put on their shoes and socks. Christopher and Thomas continue wading along in the water while the others walk along the low wall of the bank. Every time the two heroes manage to negotiate a small weir in the stream the children on the bank shout, "They've done it!"

With these happy calls, which seem to be addressed to the water itself, the children bid farewell to the stream.

The many hours spent by the children playing in the stream provide them with exciting new experiences. The characteristic of the stream — namely to carry away everything that is given to it — fascinates the children. They do not ask (yet): "Where does the stream come from, where does it go?" The quality of being alive, moving and ever-moving is one that belongs to children, too. They see how one wave follows another in never ceasing flow; when one wave has gone the next is there already. With flowing water, they are able to feel timelessness and endlessness, a continuous process eternally recurring.

The counterpart to this quality of the ever-flowing river is offered by the solid formed objects floating on the water, and herein lies the excitement. When the children set their bits of wood and their boats upon the waves, taking care that they do not come to grief, the excitement of play begins for them. If there are obstacles to the stream such as rocks, branches or limbs of trees, or a dam of leaves, will the flow come to a halt? Any kind of obstruction goes against the whole flowing nature of the water that does not want to be held up — and if it does occur it makes the children do all they can to get the water flowing again.

12. Play with Sand

How glad we are in the kindergarten that we have got a sand-pit. Though of course it would be better to let the children play with sand and water at the seaside: there water and sand mix naturally.

We must take care of the sand-pit. It should be replenished with fresh clean sand from time to time; and it should be kept covered when not in use so that it does not dry out or become too wet, and so that the sand stays clean.

On hot summer days, the young child sits in his sand-pit and lets the dry sand run through his fingers. Over and over again he picks up sand in his hands and lets it trickle out slowly. If he starts digging a hole in the sand-pit, the hole falls in because the sand has no adhesion and runs back in. Water has to be added to make this light substance stick together better. Now the sand becomes heavier and can be shaped. The cake-moulds are filled and refilled and the cakes made. Lots and lots of cakes are made, set in a row, and swept away again.

At the other end of the sand-pit, the children are making a little baking oven out of stones and boards, so that the cakes can be baked. Everyone is allowed to taste them.

A group of five- and six-year-olds have taken

complete possession of a big sand–pit. They are using their spades very adroitly and are shovelling a big sand heap together in the middle. They are going to make a tunnel through it. The construction is firmed up by eight hands patting it on all sides. They are all eagerly patting the moist warm sand. Is it really firm enough?

Next the children take their spades to dig passages under the mountain. They sit in a square opposite each other and each starts digging on his own. Before long they have got so far that their arms disappear almost up to their elbows. Then Hans calls out to his opposite number: "I can feel your spade, let's go on digging with our hands."

Both children lay their spades on one side and carry on digging and probing, and oh joy, it is not long before their hands touch. But then they can feel spades coming from the sides. Suddenly fresh sand pours into the passage as hands arrive from the direction of the other two tunnellers.

Inside the sand mountain it is becoming lighter and lighter. Now Hans lies on his tummy and peers through the passage with one eye. "I can see right through to you," he calls to his opposite number. "Put your arm into your hole, and you too, and you," till all four hands touch in the middle. But now a deep crack appears in the mountain near one of the openings, the sand begins to pour in from the top, and one half of the mountain caves in. Hans calls out woefully: "We didn't pat it hard enough!"

A whole group of children are standing in a half circle round a heap on which a ball-run has been made. Originally it had just been a sand-heap, but then the children's hands had made a run starting at the top and spiralling downwards. At the bottom of the run they dug a little pit to catch the balls.

Now the game starts. One child after the other rolls his ball down the run. If the ball gets stuck the child gives it a push. Once all the balls have landed in the pit they are shared out again.

Mark now has the idea of building a tunnel. He takes two boards and cautiously begins to build in one of the boards as a roof over the run just above the pit. After he succeeds in this he starts to build in the second board further up. Now his playmates enjoy rolling their balls under the two tunnels.

A four-year-old boy was sitting in his sand-pit in the garden digging a hole. He went on digging until he had dug a deep hole. Then he filled his pail with water and poured it into the hole. Three or four more pailfuls were quickly added until the hole was filled with water.

But the boy had hardly stirred the mixture before he could see that the water had grown less. He quickly ran to fill his pail and pour the water into the hole. But the water went on disappearing. He just could not stop it!

At the right moment his five-year-old friend appeared and watched what the younger one was doing. "Wait a moment, I'll come straight back," he called. The five-year-old disappeared into his own house and soon came back with a piece of cellophane which he spread out in the porous hole. How surprised the younger one was when the water did not disappear any more!

In this instance, the four–year–old is so taken up with what is happening that he observes everything with the greatest wonder. The five–year–old on the other hand can remember that he has seen that a leaky basin had been lined with a piece of cellophane before water had been poured in. He is able now to apply that experience on his own.

The sand–pit was suddenly turned into a garden. It was the season when the rose–hips were gleaming among the green leaves. Lena and Iris were running about in the fields. There they found a place where bluebells, daisies and buttercups were flowering. The children kept bending down and picking flowers, and now and again leaves from the bushes. Suddenly they ran to the sand–pit and squatted down in a corner. There they planted their flowers in "their garden." Very carefully they poked a hole in the sand with their fingers, put a flower stalk in and pressed the earth together just as they had seen their kindergarten teacher do when she was working in the garden. Between the flowers they laid various leaves, large and small, together with a few stones. Suddenly they stood by the rose–bush and picked the hips, then they hurried back.

Hardly had they got back before the hips came alive! They went walking among the flowers, sometimes treading on the leaves, upon which they got thrown away as a punishment! Quite unexpectedly a ladybird appeared who was greeted happily by the rose-hip children, and later when it was evening the ladybirds were laid to sleep on the softest leaves.

13. Plants, Animals and the Wind

In the hands of young children flowers come alive. Children look at flowers as if they were looking into their faces and were going to talk to them. Of course we grown-ups cannot understand anything of these conversations.

The closeness with which young children can relate to flowers can be experienced when they greet the first snowdrops in early spring. They kneel down before the little plant, holding their hands over it, making arms and hands a protective wall, so that no one will tread on them. When their arms and hands grow tired, they fetch stones to make a proper protective wall round the flowers and then the children sit beside them for a while. Only a short time ago the last snow had lain there, and it is still cold, and only now and again does the sun shine. Then suddenly this snowdrop appears and gives the children the feeling that there are many mysteries in the spring air.

It does not take very long then before the meadows are golden with dandelions, and then white with the fluffy heads. What child does not love watching the floating seeds blown off from the head! On warm summer days they float away, borne by the summer breeze, followed by the wondering gaze of the children.

For us adults it is a specially happy sight when children are allowed to pick flowers in the hayfield before the first cut is made: there go the little ones among the tall grasses, disappearing as red, yellow and blue tufts in the grass. They never grow tired of picking one flower after another, until their hands can no longer hold any more.In the end the whole glorious bunch is given to their mother: nature has given it to the child, and the child received it to pass it on.

It is important that young children should be able to take what they need for their play from where there is an abundance, for only abundance gives scope to their play–imagination and enables the child's originality to come to expression; so young children need many seeds to pour out, many cloths in many colours, many bits of wood and so on, for nature herself offers such abundance.

In autumn days when the chestnuts were falling from the trees, a group of children received a very big basket filled with these shining brown chestnuts. "Oh dear," thought the person in charge of the group. "What shall I do with all this? It's far too much." Meantime however the children were thrilled. They constructed a "potato store" under the table. Then they found a long cardboard tube which they fastened to an upturned chair. Now the "potatoes" went hurtling down this opening into the store. And a potato store has to be full or it just isn't a potato store at all! Now the group leader was delighted that she had been able to give the children such an abundance.

From her great wealth nature bestows her fruits on the children who feel themselves enriched thereby — and who show their gratitude by their happiness at play, deeply immersed in nature herself.

Every morning during the holidays four–year–old Peter runs out of the family holiday home into the wood, calling: "Mummy, I'm going 'snafting!' " Then Mother looks out of the window and sees Peter crouching under a large tree, often kneeling too, and working away among the spreading roots. Sometimes Peter laid flowers, leaves and little stones among the roots. After a long time, he comes home with a "snafter," that is a bit of root. This snafter is so important that they have to take it back with them into the town at the end of the holidays. But when the family went on holiday to a different place, Peter did not go snafting any more.

What actually is a "snafter"? What does it look like? The thing that had to be taken home at the end of the holidays looked like a little ball of root in which a lot of surface detail was woven. If we go into the sound of the word "snafter" we can feel that it means something active, living, which you can sense through the word. This should convince us that the sound has been created through the experience of something that has being. Whether the young child had experienced a gnome, a root or a tree–elemental and had "worked" with him we cannot know, we can only have an inkling. This example is not unique. For children everything in nature is alive and closely related to them. Most children do not say anything about this, perhaps because they feel that they will not be rightly understood.

For the child the forest is quite mysterious. It is so vast and deep that the child cannot fathom it. In its silent depths you can hear sounds which are only audible because of the great stillness. Suddenly there is a crack, a bird flies up, you can hear the beat of its wings, the pigeons coo, then there is another crack. When you look into the wood it goes darker and darker. The sunbeams breaking through the clouds unexpectedly light up some tree-trunks, and cast a patch of sunlight on the ground where there is a soft cushion of moss with prickly outshoots beside it.

At the edge of the forest not far from where young Peter went "snafting," he and his little friends found some overhanging bushes. The children parted the branches and sat down underneath the bushes: they needed a little house, and here they found it. But soon they came running out through the undergrowth to gather long fronds of bracken. These they strewed on the floor of their house and then lay down on the soft fronds; and so they were quite at home for a time.

Not only are water, earth and flowers, meadow and forest, all friends to the children but animals, too. Children are very fond of any animals which they are allowed to approach.

Anna, an only child, never felt lonely when her kitten kept her company, for instance on a Sunday morning long before her parents had woken up. She cared for the kitten, carried it around, put it in her play-corner and let it play with a ball of wool. How often she talked to her little companion, who always seemed to understand her. Only when she went to school and began to have other playmates, did the friendship with her kitten begin to cool down; and the kitten went back to the cushion on Anna's chair and slept most of the day.

Very small animals and creatures can also call forth the child's love. In the summertime when all the ladybirds come visiting the hedge–roses, I was able to observe children sitting in the grass watching them. The ladybirds were rapidly moving their tiny legs as they crawled over the children's arms and hands. If one of them happened to spread its wings and fly up off their fingers into the air, the children would gaze after it sympathetically for a long time.

Two seven–year–old girls had been sent along a path through the fields to the neighbouring village to deliver something to their relations there. On their way home they discovered a light brown snail without a home wandering across the path. Right away the two children decided that they had to stay by the snail until it had reached the other side of the path. At first they lay down on their tummies to watch from "a snail's height" how the little animal was progressing. It took a long time to reach half way. The children sat up, stayed quite still and did not disturb the snail until it had reached the middle. Then they began to sing softly: "Snaily, snaily, snawk, show me you can walk." Sitting cross–legged they sang the song quite a few times before the snail crossed the narrow path and had escaped all danger. Then the children continued on their way home.

Meanwhile at home the parents had begun to be anxious because the children had stayed away so long. The children were not received very kindly — but they did not feel guilty in any way, because they had only been protecting the snail from being trodden on or run over by a bicycle. How long the snail had taken to cross they did not know, nor had they any way of relating the time to the normal periods of the day. Feeling that the grown-ups had not understood them, they went off into the garden.

When young children are dealing with animals, it can be seen in the children's eyes that they have compassion on the animals, who are so narrowly constrained in their one-sidedness, above all in the one-sidedness of their movements. It is as if the children can feel the longing of the animals to be freed from their constraints.

Grown-ups must show a lot of patience on walks with their young companions. While the grown-ups may have set themselves a particular goal for their walk, their young son is less interested in the goal than in what is crawling at his feet at just that moment. He is always stopping to watch a worm, or because a beetle has just alighted on his hand or because he wants to pick a flower just off the path.

Once the family have reached a viewpoint where the parents are carried away by the beauty of the landscape, the little fellow only looks for a moment before he starts collecting the coloured stones that are lying at the edge of the path. This is because a wide expanse and distance cannot yet be taken in by young children. For them nature has to be close to, immediate and if possible also to be grasped. We grown-ups on the other hand are admirers and explorers of nature, we study her laws and try to master her. In contrast to young children who live so close to nature, we grown-ups live at a certain remove. The child lives with the ladybird, with the flowers, with the flowing of the stream. He is himself still embedded in the life-forces of nature. For him everything in field, and meadow, in forest and garden is alive, full of being and movement; everything is full of rustlings and whisperings and sighings. Completely given over to the movement of the wind, the little girl dances with outstretched arms, until she spins down to the ground, while the other children with their long brightly coloured strips of paper are running into the wind letting the wind tug at their paper so that it flies up and down.

14. Relating to Nature

Young children absorb life–forces which they can only receive from nature, for no other realm can give what nature gives. With all their bodily strength, children give themselves up to what is offered to them. Their souls become rich when they can become familiar in their play with water, earth, sand, stone, plants and animals. But nature can be a great danger, too, for young children — that is, when they are left *alone* in nature too much and for too long.

Every morning a number of small children came running out of a chalet beside a lake. They would run along the lakeside and through the meadow at the back of the house and away into the fields beyond. The wide shore stretched into the distance, strewn with all kinds of stones, large and small, and even rocks. The next house was a long way off and the shore was deserted.

As each spring brought warmer days, more and more children would gather along these shores. The children met early in the day and stayed out all morning until they were called in for their midday meal. Then the whole crowd of children could be seen wandering along the shore all afternoon, splashing in the water and often tussling with each other. No grown–up bothered about them.

"We are so glad to be able to live out here in these beautiful surroundings," the mother called to me. "It is so good for the children."

The mother could not believe that being left to themselves in this glorious nature was not at all good for the children, that they were growing wild and uncouth. After a time their playing stopped, the children were overwhelmed by the might of nature. They began to throw stones at little birds on the lake. Now and again they succeeded in hitting one of the birds. What the children lacked was the human word, human work, the activity which the child seeks in order to learn.

The second danger for the young child is inherent in our civilization, in that it makes the experience of nature foreign to man. How many gardens have already disappeared where we used to play as children or even where we let our own children play? It is becoming harder to settle down under a tree to dream, to climb into a tree to read, or to mix earth and water. Asphalt spreads further and further into nature. Children could roll their marbles on it if only it were not so dangerous!

This trend cannot be counteracted merely by providing public playgrounds, or by organized walks, for nature speaks much more spontaneously and intimately than this to the young child.

The despair which can come over children when the experience of nature is taken from them little by little — as happens in the cities when one natural playground after the other is built upon — is described in the writings of Christiane F. who spent the first happy years of her early childhood in the German countryside:*

In our village we often went by bicycle into the forest to a stream with a bridge. There we built dams and castles in the water. Sometimes everyone together, sometimes each one for himself. And if we broke it all down again it was done in agreement, and we all enjoyed it. In our village there was no leader. Anyone could make suggestions about what we should play at. It was a true children's democracy ...

We were also well prepared for rain. In the forest we gathered thick pieces of oak-bark and in bad weather we cut out our boats from it. In fine weather we built little harbours and sailed our oak-bark boats in races.

But when the family moved to the suburbs of Berlin, the child had to come to terms with enormous changes in her life. This was made easier at first because she was allowed to keep her beloved animals: four mice, two cats, two rabbits, a budgerigar and Agar, the brown bulldog, who slept beside her bed at night. Even in the city as it was then, she discovered that "there were still remnants of nature. We would bicycle with our dogs. We played on the old refuse dumps which had been covered with earth. Our dogs always played with us. 'Tracker-dog' was our favourite game. One person would hide while his dog was held fast. Then the dog had to go and find him. My Agar had the best nose." Soon afterwards a pony riding-school was built near this playground and "the

* The following extracts are from *Christiane F.*

last bit of free nature was fenced in." But Christiane could still go riding there now and again whenever she had enough pocket-money, and she could help in the stables.

Then she describes how notices saying "Protected Green Area" appeared on every strip of grass in the district forbidding the children to play there. One day Christiane went for a walk with her dog, Agar. On the way she wanted to pick some flowers for her mother, as she often did. All she could find were some stunted little roses which she tried to pick, pricking her fingers in the process. She had not yet quite taken in what "Protected Green Area" meant. The warden made a big fuss, and reported the child to her parents. And for this childlike act of picking flowers for her mother, Christiane's father gave her a thrashing.

In the summer the children wanted to play at marbles — but where? In the sand-pit it was not possible because it did not have a hard enough floor. At last they found an ideal marble-run. "Underneath the sycamore trees a round opening in the asphalt had been left, which had been filled with firm clean earth. It was just ideal for marbles." But as often as the children became absorbed in their play with their marbles, they were driven away by the gardener or by the warden, until finally the earth was dug over and a stop put to the game.

Even the "Adventure Playground" which had been temporarily erected had such strict rules that it could not satisfy the children's needs. It was soon closed again.

For that we children now got a real attraction. The

authorities built a toboggan hill. It was wonderful that first winter. We were allowed to choose our own runs down the "mountain" ... The days with snow belong to my happiest days in Gropiusstadt. In spring it was nearly as much fun. We played there with our dogs and rolled down the slopes. The best was whizzing round on our bikes.

But soon we were forbidden to play on the toboggan hill. A wall was built round it. Asphalt paths crossed nearly all the runs. Only one strip of grass remained as a toboggan–run.

Everything surrounding the new suburb now became more and more "improved." Up to that time, the children could reach really wonderful playgrounds only a short distance away. For instance they discovered a wood which they called "No man's land." Trees, bushes, grass, as tall as the children, old planks and water–holes. The children climbed, played hide and seek, felt like explorers, made camp–fires, baked potatoes and were able to make smoke signals. But soon the guardians of order burst into this paradise, put up "No Entry" notices and made sure that order was kept.

Finally, the children escaped out to fields that were no longer cultivated; there corn, grass, nettles and poppies were still growing. But even here their luck did not last: before very long the developers built tennis–courts on the open spaces where the children came to breathe in the scent of the flowers of the field.

Two great dangers threaten children equally today: firstly, the danger of growing wild because of being left alone too much, above all in the artificial village life of our modern suburbs; and secondly the lack of opportunities, as the town encroaches, to play in an open and natural landscape. Both are dangers which, as in Christiane's case, ultimately impoverish the child's soul and can lead to an unbalanced and unhappy later life.

A happy healthy feeling for life, the joy of playing and experiencing the elements, the intimate conversations of the child with animals, plants and trees: all of this makes up the life-world of children in which they can unfold their soul. We adults, too, should endeavour especially to regain the fullness of this life-world.

Conclusion

My reader, I am sure, knows that unswerving gaze of a young child looking at you as if to see right into your heart. This open gaze, untouched as yet by self-consciousness, expresses boundless trust. How can we, as adults, do justice to this trust?

Of course parental love and devotion is very important. But equally important is the respect we show for the child's personality. The young child wants to be taken seriously just as the adult takes himself and his own activity seriously. That is why the adult should watch a child's play with the greatest interest, realizing that for children their play is just as important as work is for the adult. We can see how great is the child's application when they are playing, how they stint neither effort nor trouble.

When for example the five-year-old is going to perform a puppet-play for the rest of the family, there are such a lot of preparations. First they have to set up the stage on the table and fix the curtain. Then they have to gather all the props and everything else that is needed and lay it all out in order. Then they go on to put the chairs in a row and get the puppets ready. They may go out of their way to find a child's trumpet in order to announce the beginning of the play. Only when everything is perfectly ready, will the play begin.

Just as earnestly and busily other children will play the part of parent to the toys or dolls, caring for them with the greatest devotion. They will arrange the toy house with love and care, finding furniture, cloths, cushions and chairs. They will make little beds, even a baby's bottle out of a piece of wood. Many more examples could be given. Such observations show how very important it is to encourage the child at play.

Parents and teachers often say that children who have discovered how to play in their pre–school days transform their love of play into eagerness to learn when they go up to school. The play of their early years has become a work–activity which leads to real joy and pleasure in life.

Dotty Turner Coplen

Parenting
a Path through
Childhood

Combining her experience as a mother and grand-
mother with her studies in psychology and social
work, the author presents a warm and human way of
understanding the nature and needs of children.
Parents and professionals working with children will
find this a helpful book for understanding the needs of
children, developing an awareness of their individual
differences and observing how behaviour is learned.

Floris Books

Heidi Britz–Crecelius

Children at Play
Preparation for Life

Play is more vital for the child's future than many
parents realize. Children's fantasies should be allowed
free scope, for they are learning through play and the
spontaneous creations of their own magical worlds.
The more they can be absorbed in their play, the more
fully and effectively they later take their place in the
world of adults. This book offers many practical
suggestions especially for the urban family. Dozens of
real children play through the pages of this book
making it a delight to read and its conclusions con-
vincing. It is a refreshing and a timely warning for a
technological age.

Floris Books